LUTON HOO

THE WERNHER COLLECTION

ABOVE: *The SW wing from the rose garden. The gardens were laid out over 70 years ago, the park having previously reached right to the house. In spring the rock garden (a short distance from the house) is rich with rhododendron and azalea, while in autumn an extensive display of dahlias is planted below the top terrace.* FACING PAGE: *The portico, erected by Smirke, on completing the entrance front in about 1830. Robert Adam's design of 1766–7 had not been completely carried out.*

The English Room

The first room is devoted to English pictures of the 18th century when the English School, led by Reynolds and Gainsborough, took the lead in European painting. One exception is the portrait of *Queen Anne When Young*, hanging over the fireplace (*right*), and attributed to Willem Wissing (1655–1687), the pupil of Sir Peter Lely. It was formerly attributed to Lely himself as a portrait of Nell Gwyn; the latter attribution was impossible, since the ermine-bordered robe depicts a woman of royal or noble lineage, which Nell Gwyn was not. Of several works by John Hoppner (1758/9–1810) the finest is the charming child portrait of the *Hon. Henrietta Hanbury-Tracy* illustrated below (*right*). Hoppner, at his best with children, is here seen at his most successful; his young sitter was a daughter to the first Lord Sudeley, one of Queen Victoria's Coronation peers in 1838. This room also contains a portrait of *Mrs. Grace* (*below*), one of the rare easel pictures by Richard Cosway (1742–1821), best known for his charming miniatures. There is also an excellent example by the comparatively unknown Francis Abbott (*c.* 1760–1803), a portrait of *Admiral Sir Edmund Affleck*, who distinguished himself under the more famous Admiral Lord Rodney in the West Indies. A small topographical landscape is the *Cow at Kenwood, Middlesex*, painted in 1797 by Julius Caesar Ibbetson (1759–1817) for the Countess of Mansfield, whose home was at Kenwood; it shows the house, with its pedimented front, in the background.

LUTON HOO

M. Urwick Smith, MA, AMA, *Curator*

AMONG the splendid country houses that have been opened to the public since the war, it is doubtful if any can display an art collection as superb, in point both of importance and variety, as Luton Hoo. Chatsworth, for instance, the *chef d'oeuvre* of the architect Talman, can claim the distinction of an incomparably fine house, containing the accumulated treasures of generations of the Cavendish family. At Luton Hoo, where the Adam-designed house itself has been spoilt by successive fires and drastic alterations, the emphasis is essentially on the contents. This is due primarily to Sir Julius Wernher, who collected the main part of them.

Yet Luton Hoo has a past as historic as most. Although not mentioned in Domesday Book (1086) there has been a manor house here from at least the 13th century, when the de Hoo family was in occupation. In fact it is likely that the site had seen some form of occupation since prehistoric times—as a hill-top it would have been a likely site for a pagan grove. On a site near the southern edge of the estate a Roman sarcophagus was discovered in 1843 and is now in the British Museum, whilst a hoard of Roman coins dating from Caracalla, A.D. 211, to Claudius Gothicus, A.D. 270, was found close to the house itself in 1862.

The name "Hoo" is a Saxon word meaning the spur of a hill, and is commonly found in the south-east Midlands and East Anglia. The de Hoos, the first family associated with Luton Hoo, were in possession by the middle of the 13th century, and evidently took their name from the property they held, as commonly occurred in the Middle Ages. Comparatively undistinguished during their three centuries of ownership, the last of the family achieved greater fame, and was created Lord Hoo and Hastings in 1448, dying without male heirs seven years later. It is interesting to note that one of his daughters and co-heirs, Anne, married Sir Geoffrey Boleyn, Lord Mayor of London, and by him became the great-grandmother of Anne Boleyn, the second wife of King Henry VIII, and mother of Queen Elizabeth I. In fact the Boleyn family held their portion of Luton Hoo until about 1523—to within 10 years of the great queen's birth.

From then until 1601 Luton Hoo was held by families of little note, but in the latter year it was purchased by Sir Robert Napier. Napier (otherwise Sandys), the son of an Exeter merchant, appears to have been descended from the Napiers of Merchistoun in Scotland. Certainly he belonged to one of those families who enriched themselves during the Tudor period by commerce, investing their wealth in landed estates. King James I, meeting him in 1605, appears at least to have been impressed by his wealth, as the impecunious monarch noted that he might negotiate a loan with "Mr. Robert Sandiz" (as he called him). He in fact stayed at Luton Hoo in 1611, and knighted Napier in that year, and created him a baronet in the same year; this may well have been Napier's reward for financial aid. In 1612 Napier purchased from Sir John Rotherham the lordship of the manor of Luton, a lordship that has been held with the ownership of Luton Hoo until the present time.

The Napiers were a comparatively unimportant family, undistinguished even for their family connections. The last baronet, Sir John, dying in 1748, left Luton Hoo to his aunt, Frances Napier, of Harrow, who in turn left it to Francis Herne, M.P. for Bedford town, three years later. He sold the estate in 1762 for £94,700 to John Stuart, 3rd Earl of Bute, and it is through him that the Luton Hoo we know begins to emerge.

Bute, formerly tutor to King George III, became Prime Minister soon after the young king's succession to the throne in 1760; his incapacity and unpopularity led to his downfall by 1763. Bute, though no statesman, was in fact a man of culture, and settling at Luton Hoo he engaged Robert Adam, the great architect of his day, to build him a new house in place of the old one, regardless of expense. The plans were magnificent, but as often occurred with great houses, they were not completely carried out. In the end, Adam transformed much of the old house, including an incomparable suite of rooms, with a new exterior to mask the old. Work commenced in 1767, and after the set-back of a fire in 1771, was evidently well forward by 1774, for Mrs. Delany, the indefatigable visitor to many country houses,

Continued on page 5

*

RIGHT: Wooded Landscape *by Hobbema (1638-1709), one of the finest of the Dutch landscape painters. Diffused with subtle gradations of light, pictures such as this influenced Gainsborough and the English landscapists in the 18th century, and the Norwich School somewhat later.*

The Dutch Room

This room is chiefly devoted to Dutch pictures of the 17th century. The northern, Protestant, provinces of the Low Countries developed a school of painting depicting their own homeland and people. The Dutch landscapists are represented not only by the Hobbema *Wooded Landscape* (illustrated on page 3), but also by Isaac van Ostade's important *Halt at an Inn* depicted (*right*) hanging above the Louis XV lacquered commode with rich ormolu mounts of *c.* 1750. *The Palace at Brussels* by van der Heyden (1637–1712) is a topographical landscape depicting the old palace of the Dukes of Burgundy on the site of which stands Brussels' present royal palace, whilst *A Hawking Party among Ruins* by Wouwermans (1619–1668) is romantic genre. Many Dutch artists excelled in painting their countrymen at their daily pursuits, from the rich upper classes to the poorest peasants in cottage and tavern. Among these was Pieter de Hooch (1629–after 1684) with his important *Dutch Interior*, also Gabriel Metsu (1629–1667), who painted *Gentleman and a Lady at the Harpsicord (above right)*, skilfully depicting the rich fabrics of his wealthy sitters. The strongly contrasted light and shade in the picture reflects the influence of Rembrandt (1606–1669), perhaps the greatest of all Dutch painters, here represented by three characteristic portraits. Rembrandt's influence also appears in *The Good Housewife* attributed to Gerard Dou (1613–1675), who worked in his studio, and was Metsu's master. The only other Dutch portrait in the Collection is *Head of a Boy* by Frans Hals (1580–1666) *(above)*. Hals, best known for his roistering sitters with their splendid panache, is here represented by an extremely sensitive study, yet handled in characteristic style. The painters of peasant life are represented by Adriaen van Ostade and the sea by Willem van de Velde the younger, whose yacht fires a salute as some (evidently) distinguished visitors are pulled away in the barge to left.

visiting Luton Hoo that year, states that "the house, tho' not entirely finished according to the plan, is very handsome and convenient". She adds that in each room a screen stood beside the fireplace "with ye plan of ye room, and with the names of the hands by whom the pictures were painted, in order as they stand".

Dr. Johnson, visiting Luton Hoo with Boswell in 1781, was particularly laudatory, saying: "This is one of the places I do not regret having come to see. It is a very stately place indeed. In the house magnificence is not sacrificed to convenience, nor convenience to magnificence. The Library is very splendid, the dignity of the rooms is very great, and the quantity of pictures is beyond expectation, beyond hope".

The interiors of the principal rooms were, indeed, splendid. Of these the Library was the finest of all, Adam himself considering it his "*chef d'oeuvre* both in point of elegance and contrivance". It extended 146 feet—the length of the ground floor on the south wing—being three rooms joined by folding doors, the ceiling painted by Cipriani. Bute's library was famous, apart from its architecture, and was considered by many to be second only to Blenheim. The rooms contained not only a collection of about 30,000 books, but mathematical and scientific instruments of great interest. Above the bookcases hung some of the larger and more important pictures, for which Luton Hoo also became noted. Another splendid room, the Saloon (now the Dining Room), was considered "as delightful as silk furniture, immense mirrors and excellent pictures, can make it". Bute married a daughter to the redoubtable Lady Mary Wortley Montague, a great character in her time and now chiefly famous for her correspondence. Luton Hoo contained two cabinets that had been given her by the King of Sardinia.

While Adam was altering and beautifying the house, "Capability" Brown was enlarging and landscaping the park. From a small park of about 300 acres he extended it to 1,200, later somewhat enlarged again. By damming the River Lea in two places he constructed two lakes, the larger of which, nearly a quarter of a mile in length, covers 60 acres. The smaller, of serpentine shape, is separated from the larger by a richly-timbered island. Although much of the park has been subsequently altered, with Victorian plantations of cedar and other coniferous trees, it still remains a noble example of an 18th century layout.

If the splendours of the park have survived, those of the house have unfortunately vanished. Bute's great-grandson, the 2nd Marquess of Bute, who succeeded to the property in 1814, engaged Smirke to make extensive alterations some years later, when the façade appears to have been completed similar to its present form (except the south front, which was not touched). Then in 1843 occurred the disastrous fire in which almost all was destroyed. Certain of the pictures, part of the library, and some other things were saved; everything else was destroyed by the flames. After the fire the Bute family relinquished Luton Hoo, and the estate was sold in 1848 to John Shaw Leigh, a wealthy Liverpool solicitor with a fortune made out of building sites around the growing city. He rebuilt the house, making little alteration to the façade, which had been shored up after the fire. The Chapel, now the Main Gallery, was constructed by Street during the 1870s out of a portion of the house that had remained a shell since the 2nd Marquess of Bute's alterations of 50 years previously. Luton Hoo ultimately passed to Leigh's daughter-in-law who subsequently married, in 1883, His Excellency M. Christian de Falbe, Danish Ambassador to England; her eccentricities were long remembered in the neighbourhood of Luton.

On the death of Mme de Falbe the Leigh family also in their turn relinquished Luton Hoo, in 1903. That year was a great landmark with the purchase of the estate by Sir Julius Wernher. It saw the commencement of the present regime at Luton Hoo, and the development of the collection of works of art it now contains (although not all were originally housed here); it also commenced the transition of the house to its present architectural and decorative form.

Sir Julius Wernher, whose family records reach back to 1560, was the son of an engineer, his father having been a close friend of George and Robert Stephenson, of railway fame. Sir Julius emigrated to South Africa in 1871, and quickly became associated with the diamond-mining industry, then only in its infancy. He realised that the stones were uneconomically

ABOVE: Coronation of the Virgin, *with censing angels; left half of a diptych, French, 14th century, $5\frac{3}{4}''$ high; a charming example of the French and German ivories in the Collection.*

*

mined and engaged British mining experts to assist the industry's development. The venture was a great success and the firm of Wernher, Beit & Co. was founded, now known as the Central Mining and Investment Corporation. During these years Sir Julius was the friend of Cecil Rhodes and Mr. Asquith (later Earl of Oxford), among others famous at that period, and became one of the only five life governors of the company of De Beers. He was created a baronet in 1905.

Some years before this Sir Julius commenced his great art collection, wherein he was somewhat in advance of a number of the great American collectors, such as Pierpont Morgan, and it is through his art collection, perhaps, that he is now chiefly remembered in this country. His shrewd discernment for the finest examples is manifested in Luton Hoo. But Sir Julius was an international figure, whose collection reflects this international background as well as the art fashions of his day. He collected pictures and tapestries, and the various things the visitor expects to find in an

English country house. What is unexpected, however, is the incomparable collection of medieval ivories, Renaissance jewels and bronzes, German silver-gilt, Limoges enamels and Italian maiolica. Their quality and number are both outstanding, and the visitor must explore the Victoria and Albert Museum or other national collections to see anything comparable. This is the more remarkable as Sir Julius was able to devote but little time to collecting. Many of his purchases were made abroad.

Like other great collectors of the 19th century—for instance Sir Richard Wallace, founder of the Wallace Collection, and John Bowes, founder of the Bowes Museum at Barnard Castle—Sir Julius followed the penchant of his time in collecting French furniture and *objets d'art*, and there are splendid French tapestries at Luton Hoo, illustrated in this book. His interests extended far less to English art works; it was in fact a time when much English furniture, porcelain and silver were regarded rather as "antiques" than as works of art. Sir Julius, however, made one splendid English acquisition in 1893 with Reynolds' *Lady Caroline Price*, illustrated on page 19.

The English porcelain at Luton Hoo belonged to Sir Julius's wife. In 1888 he married Alice Sedgwick Manciewicz (who married secondly, in 1919, the late Lord Ludlow), and the collecting of English porcelain was her lifelong hobby. Consisting largely of Chelsea, Bow and Worcester porcelain, it is not a representative collection, but the quality of many of the pieces constitutes its prime importance.

Sir Julius died in 1912, leaving Luton Hoo to his wife for her life; she died in 1945 when their son, Sir Harold Wernher, came into possession. Between Sir Julius's purchase of the estate in 1903 and Sir Harold's succession, great changes took place in the house. The prevailing tastes of 1903 would scarcely have favoured a Georgian house with Victorian decorations, and Sir Julius altered it drastically, imposing continental-style casements in place of the original sash windows, and adding the attic floor, thus dwarfing the great portico. The terrace front (illustrated on page 1), the last of Adam's work to survive intact, was also altered to its present form. The principal rooms in the house were transformed in the French style, as they may now be seen, and the Grand Stairs inserted. The marble walls in the Dining Room were erected specially to frame the Beauvais tapestries, which have never since been moved. These alterations were completed by 1907, and now reflect the profuse grandeur of the Edwardian period.

During the present century life at Luton Hoo has not passed undisturbed. In the First World War it was used as an Army Headquarters and then as a Military Convalescent Home for Officers. In the last war it became the headquarters of Eastern Command. After derequisitioning, Sir Harold and Lady Zia Wernher returned here as their home. They then decided to make the greater part of their art collection available to visitors during the summer months each year, and the house has consequently undergone further changes to provide a home for its owners and a setting for their incomparable possessions. To Luton Hoo Sir Harold brought further items to enhance the collection. For instance he made good the paucity of English furniture (notably the globe bureau, lower corridor) and further enriched the collection of Dutch pictures, e.g. *The Wooded Landscape* by Hobbema illustrated on page 3.

In 1917 Sir Harold married Lady Anastasia (Zia) Mikhailovna Torby, elder daughter to the late Grand Duke Michael of Russia and Countess de Torby, and it is Lady Zia who has contributed to Luton Hoo her collection of the work of Carl Fabergé. The Grand Duke Michael was a grandson of the Emperor Nicholas I of Russia, who was emperor on the outbreak of the Crimean War in 1854, and the great-great-grandson of Catherine the Great. He at one time lived at Kenwood, Middlesex, another house altered by Adam in 1767–68 for the 1st Earl of Mansfield, the great lawyer. For a few years, until 1754, before either the alterations there or his purchase of Luton Hoo, Kenwood belonged to Lord Bute. The lacquered bureau, in the Dutch Room, together with the wine cooler illustrated on page 18, were once part of the Mansfields' possessions there. Lady Zia's maternal great-grandfather was Alexander Sergeivitch Pushkin, the Russian poet.

In the Russian and Photograph Rooms is a collection of portraits of the Russian Imperial Family, ranging from Christian, Duke of Anhalt-Zerbst (the father of Catherine the Great) to the last Czar, Nicholas II, assassinated 1918. A group of miniatures was recently (1960) given to Lady Zia by the family of the late Grand Duchess Xenia (a sister to the last Czar, and aunt by marriage to Lady Zia); they include one of her great-grandmother, the Empress Alexandra Feodorovna, who was a sister to William I, first German Emperor. Another larger miniature, by the same artist, Winberg, shows her in a stupendous jewelled head-dress. The Russian court-dresses are of outstanding magnificence, particularly the maid-of-honour's dress in red velvet embroidered with gold sequins, left to Lady Zia Wernher by Mme Poklewska-Koziel; also the pink dress, formerly worn by her mother, the late Baroness de Stoëckl. There is also a

pale blue brocaded dress believed worn by Lady Zia Wernher's mother, the late Countess de Torby, for Queen Victoria's Diamond Jubilee celebrations, 1897.

Luton Hoo is here emphasised as an historic monument and museum rather than as a home. Yet a home it has always been and it is hoped it will long remain so. During the difficult years of the 20th century the opening of the house to the public has invested it with new interest, and has helped to surmount the problems that now face all owners of such properties. But the opening of country houses to the public, although frowned upon during the 19th century, is nothing new. During the 18th century country house visiting was a feature of a tour through Britain. Jane Austen exemplifies this when she takes Elizabeth Bennet with her aunt and uncle on their fateful visit to Pemberley in *Pride and Prejudice*.

Among the many distinguished visitors to Luton Hoo was the late Queen Mary; it was during a visit here in 1891 that she became first engaged to the Duke of Clarence (the eldest son of King Edward VII), whose untimely death occurred so shortly afterwards. Years later she was the first visitor to the Collection immediately before its opening. Since that occasion great numbers of people have yearly visited Luton Hoo, and it is hoped great numbers more will long have the facility to do so.

The Ivory Room

Ivory, once highly valued, is now rarely used as a medium of fine art. This collection, the most important private collection of its kind in Britain, comprises chiefly religious ivories, from Byzantine work of the 10th century to French work of the 14th—the finest century of European ivories. The triptyches and other religious pieces were used as aids to devotion and the meditative religious life of the Middle Ages. Besides religion, ivory was also used for secular work, and mirror cases and other trinkets are displayed in the room. Also displayed here are the two wings from a rare English ivory triptych, of which the centre plaque belongs to the Victoria and Albert Museum; during the 19th century it was not, unfortunately, uncommon for pieces of this kind to be divided among more than one collector, though in this case it is unknown when the vandalism took place. On an early Italo-Byzantine ivory plaque the Death of the Virgin has been depicted.

TOP LEFT: *Polyptych, with* The Virgin and Child *in the centre compartment; such ivories were mounted on wooden bases for use as portable altars; French, 14th century.*

TOP RIGHT: *Diptych with* The Crucifixion *and* The Virgin in Glory*—the Virgin crowned by a flying angel; French, 14th century.*

ABOVE: *Pastoral staff,* The Virgin in Glory (The Crucifixion *on the other side*), *also with traces of colouring; French, 14th century.*

FACING PAGE: *Figure of* St. Catherine of Alexandria, *standing on the head of the Emperor Maxentius, an outstanding ivory of French workmanship of about 1400, which is 4 inches in height.*

The Blue Hall

Formerly the Entrance Hall, the Blue Hall stands in the very centre of the house, and here for the first time the visitor sees the ornate French decorations introduced by Sir Julius Wernher. The rich effect is enhanced by the magnificent contents of the room. Foremost among them are some of the French tapestries for which Luton Hoo is famous. The *Chancellerie* (*left*) was woven at Gobelins with the arms of France and Navarre, and in the corners those (later) of Louis Phelypeaux, Duc de la Vrillière, foreign minister to King Louis XV. Below it stands part of a suite of eight armchairs and sofa, covered in Beauvais tapestry illustrating scenes from the fables of La Fontaine to designs of Jean Baptiste Oudry; of Louis XVI period, they are about 1780 in date. On either side of the door leading to the corridor are four more Gobelins tapestries illustrating *Les Mois Grotesques*, designed by Claude Audran early in the 18th century. On either side of the fireplace are two cases of Sèvres porcelain, the royal porcelain manufactory of France. Among the Sèvres are two plates from a service ordered by Catherine the Great of Russia in 1778 (*below*), bearing the royal monogram EII, in flowers, for *Ekaterina II.* The service consists of over 700 pieces and is mostly still in Russia. A Sèvres ewer and basin (*below left*) in an unusual shade of rose bears the date-letter H for 1760 and is brilliantly painted with flowers by Tandart. The pair of plates in bleu-du-roi, decorated with scenes from Ovid's *Metamorphoses,* are from a service ordered by Louis XVI in 1783, to comprise 445 pieces, but never completed owing to the onset of the French Revolution. The completed portion belongs to H.M. The Queen.

ABOVE: *Group of flower sprays. These decorative pieces are only a few inches in height. Most remarkable is the gypsophila, which consists of a gold stalk with many soldered off-shoots, set with tiny diamonds, and growing from a vase of nephrite. The rest are set in rock crystal, hollowed to simulate water in a vase, from which the sprays are removable. There are two sprays of forget-me-not, the larger composed of turquoise clusters with diamond centres, the smaller in enamel. The lilies-of-the-valley are composed of pearls with nephrite leaves. The strawberry plant in translucent enamels bears a flower in pearls and rose diamonds.*

BELOW LEFT: *Cigarette box, in gold decorated with translucent green enamel. The lid, surmounted by a Russian eagle in diamonds, frames miniatures of Nicholas II and the Empress Alexandra Feodorovna. Said to have been presented to the Czar in 1913, it would rank among the numerous pieces made by Fabergé to commemorate the tercentenary of the Romanov dynasty. The Empress, a princess of Hesse, was a grand-daughter to Queen Victoria.*

Peter Carl Fabergé

Fabergé, whose main workshop with its large international staff of assistants was in St. Petersburg, was jeweller to Alexander III and Nicholas II, the two last czars of Russia, between 1881 and 1917. Although a jeweller in the usual sense, his finest work consisted of the small gold, enamelled and jewelled objects largely made for the Russian Imperial Family and their friends. Nicholas II himself took a personal interest in these productions, especially the Easter Eggs, containing a "surprise", presents for the Empress and his mother, the Dowager Empress, each year.

Among Fabergé's patrons were Lady Zia Wernher's parents, the late Grand Duke Michael of Russia and Countess de Torby, from whom Lady Zia had inherited most of the collection. Fabergé's emphasis was less on splendour than on design and the finest craftsmanship and materials. The cigarette cases and electric bell pushes, parasol handles and scent bottles, rely on the various coloured golds, the quality and colouring of the enamels, and the matching of small but perfectly set stones, for their effect. In these days it is difficult to realise that most of them were made for daily use.

TOP LEFT: *Tray in nephrite (Russian jade), the gold handles decorated in the style of Louis XV, with translucent strawberry enamel, and rose diamonds. This in one of the largest pieces made by Fabergé, whose work was mostly on a miniature scale; it measures 17½ inches in length, the diameter of the tray being 10½ inches.*

CENTRE LEFT: *Notecase in green jasper elaborately decorated in gold and rose diamonds, with a brilliant diamond thumb-piece. The gold pencil is set with a jasper cameo of a warrior, and the case lining and notebook are in yellow silk. This piece is in the Louis XV style, which Fabergé occasionally imitated.*

BELOW LEFT: *Animals in nephrite and obsidian, the eyes set with precious stones. The frog is a parasol handle and the fish an electric bell push.*

FACING PAGE, TOP LEFT: *Freedom box in nephrite with red and green gold mounts, the lid surmounted by the Russian Eagle in mat and polished yellow gold. It was given by Nicholas II to the 14th Earl of Pembroke, when the latter was attached to the Emperor's suite during a visit to Queen Victoria at Balmoral in 1896.*

ABOVE: *Another view of the Blue Hall, showing the cabinets of Sèvres porcelain on either side of the fireplace—itself one of the ornate decorative features introduced into the house by Sir Julius Wernher. The cabinets display the porcelain described and illustrated on page 8 and, among other pieces, an important vase in a rare blue colour only known to have been used in 1767 and 1768 (left-hand cabinet).*

BELOW: *Two examples of silver-gilt; one of a pair of early 18th century German sideboard dishes, 24 inches in diameter (left), and (right) cup and cover by Paul Lamerie, 1750. The silver-gilt and tapestries are described overleaf.*

The Dining Room

The Dining Room is a further instance of the elaborate French decorations at Luton Hoo. Here marble, gilding and cut glass combine to achieve a sparkling richness. More natural is the panoramic view of the park seen from the windows, overlooking the Lea valley with the larger of the lakes below. It is hard to realise that the railway line from Luton to London runs through the trees on the far side of the lake. The most striking feature of the room itself, off-setting the sparkle by a contrasting softness, is the set of Beauvais tapestries, *The Story of the King of China.* The original set was woven early in the 18th century for the Comte de Toulouse (son of Louis XIV and Mme de Montespan) to decorate the Château de Rambouillet. The complete set should consist of six tapestries, though no such complete set is known to survive. The fact that the Luton Hoo set was rolled up for many years accounts for its remarkable brilliance.

ABOVE: *The Audience* tapestry.

FACING PAGE: The Dining Room. The table is laid for dessert, and the side tables are set with magnificent silver-gilt, which is gold plated on silver. Much of it, together with the cut glass, is of royal origin. For instance, the candlesticks and candelabra (London, 1753, with additions 1806–9), the knives, forks and spoons (London, 1806–7), and the wine coasters and labels (London, 1805–6) all belonged to the Duke of Cumberland, the son of King George III who became King of Hanover in 1837, when the Salic Law prevented Queen Victoria from succeeding her uncle, William IV, on the Hanoverian throne.

The sideboard dishes and ewers on the end side table (illustrated on the previous page) also belonged to the Duke of Cumberland; they descended to him from the Elector of Hanover who became King George I of England in 1714. They are by Conrad Hollings of Hanover and are engraved with the Elector's arms flanked by his initials GL, for George Lewis. The Dresden-handled dessert knives and forks in the left-hand window case also belonged to the Duke of Cumberland, whilst the dessert plates (London, mid-18th century, decorated *c.* 1820) belonged to his brother, the Duke of Sussex.

The tray standing between the Hanoverian dishes is an important work by the Huguenot Pierre Harache, 1695, perhaps engraved by Simon Gribelin. On the other side tables is part of a mid-19th century Russian silver-gilt dinner service, copied from the original given by Catherine the Great to her favourite, Orloff. The cut glass, probably emanating from the Imperial glass manufactory at St. Petersburg, bears the monogram EM for the Grand Duchess Elizabeth Mikhailovna, a grand-daughter to the Emperor Paul I. In 1844 she married Adolph, Duke of Nassau, afterwards Grand Duke of Luxembourg, and died the following year. Grand Duke Adolph was elder half-brother to Lady Zia Wernher's maternal grandfather, Prince Nicholas of Nassau.

The Marble Hall

The Marble Hall and Grand Stairs are yet a further example of Sir Julius Wernher's French decorations, and make an impressive appearance with the curved sweep of the stairs. The staircase, also French workmanship, is of wrought iron with gilt-bronze enrichments. Bergonzoli's statue, *The Love of Angels* (*facing page*), is a representation of Cupid and Psyche. Displayed in the Marble Hall are the Renaissance bronzes, mostly Italian. At first many small bronzes were deliberate fakes, intended to pass as Roman antiquities, but they quickly won a position as works of art in themselves, many of the best and simplest being superb examples of miniature statuary. Among the finest is an exquisite small plaque of the *Virgin and Child* from the workshop of Donatello (1386–1466). Many bronzes have a classical inspiration, like the magnificent *Shouting Horseman* from the studio of Riccio (1470–1532), *illustrated left*. Both are in the centre case. In the left-hand case is a 16th century bronze of Michael Angelo's *Night*, cast after his marble figure in the Medici Chapel in Florence. Most splendid of all is surely Riccio's large incense-burner (centre case) over 20″ high, the domed lid surmounted by a seated satyr holding a syrinx (pan-pipes). Among the non-Italian bronzes *The Martyrdom of St. Sebastian*, on the Upper Corridor, is a rare example of about 1500. By its very material, bronze lends itself to dramatic subjects.

*

ABOVE LEFT: *Lady Wernher, afterwards Lady Ludlow, by J. S. Sargent (1856–1925).*

ABOVE RIGHT: *Sir Julius Wernher, painted in 1912, the year of his death, by Hubert von Herkomer (1849–1914). It was Sir Julius who transformed Luton Hoo to its present appearance, and collected most of the treasures it now contains.*

For the English porcelain collection, refer to the following pages.

ABOVE: *Pair of figures of Turkish women in early Chelsea porcelain,* c. *1750. They are based on engravings by Ravenet after drawings by François Boucher, modelled by Willems, and are believed unique; they stand 10½ inches in height and the lower figure bears the rare violet anchor mark. Their comparative simplicity contrasts with the profuse decoration and gilding of the following decade.*

ABOVE, LEFT: *Large Worcester vase, reserved panels transfer-printed with ruins, coloured by hand.*

BELOW, LEFT: *Early Derby "Chinese" group, c. 1750, representing the sense of smell.*

TOP: *Pair of magnificent Derby figures,* The Abyssinian Archers.

ABOVE: *Pair of Bow peacocks, superbly modelled and coloured.*

FACING PAGE, ABOVE: *Three large Worcester vases;* left and right, *a pair, dark blue ground, gilded, continuous hunting scenes within "gothick" panels; unsigned, but painted by J. H. O'Neale; square mark; height 20½";* centre, *dark blue ground,* A Sheep-Shearing *painted by Donaldson and signed in monogram; flower painting on reverse; the lid painted by J. H. O'Neale; square mark; height 21½".*

RIGHT: *Chelsea porcelain clock in mazarine blue and gold, the seated figure holding a ballad inscribed: "Sung by Miss Young at Ranelagh" referring either to Cecilia Young, who married Thomas Arne, the composer, or to her sister, Isabella, who performed at Ranelagh.*

The Ludlow Collection

The three rooms opening from the Upper Corridor, originally the State Suite, are now devoted to Lady Ludlow's collection of English porcelain. They consisted of a bedroom with dressing room, right, and boudoir, left.

The first room is devoted to Chelsea and Bow. The Chelsea factory (*c.* 1745–1769) was incomparably the finest in England, and to Chelsea belong many of the main pieces in the collection. An entire cabinet is given to the brilliant claret ground evolved there; this is an outstanding feature. The part tea service on the second shelf from the top with "Chinese" figures, is among England's finest porcelain accomplishments. Contemporary with Chelsea was the Bow factory, less magnificent, though often naïvely charming at its best, as exemplified in a number of the figures.

The right-hand room is devoted solely to Worcester, founded in 1751, the only English 18th century porcelain factory surviving to the present day. Here the influence of Sèvres is displayed in the decorative schemes and ground colours; the rarest is the "scale yellow", in which some charming cups and saucers and a tea-caddy are executed. A pair of double-handled cups and saucers in "scale blue" is decorated with Chinese figures by the same (unknown) hand which painted the Chelsea claret service.

The left-hand room contains a small collection of Derby, hard-paste porcelain from Plymouth and Bristol, and a few 19th century pieces from Spode, Rockingham, Swansea and Nantgarw; also 19th century Staffordshire pottery figures and animals.

The Upper and Lower Corridors and Brown Jack Room

The Upper Corridor is chiefly devoted to German silver-gilt of the 16th and 17th centuries. Here the sophisticated work of the craftsmen of Nuremberg and Augsburg contrasts sharply with the German stoneware of the same period in the other cabinets. An outstanding example of the former is the large tazza *(facing page, below left)* depicting scenes from the life of the Emperor Augustus, surmounted by a figure of Nero. This belongs to a set of 12, illustrating the lives of the Roman Emperors, originally belonging to Cardinal Aldobrandini, afterwards Pope Clement VIII, late in the 16th century. The tazzas were subsequently dispersed and not all bear the correct figure. Also on the Upper Corridor is the large tapestry, *Perseus with the Gorgon's Head;* it would have been one of a set, illustrating the story of Perseus, and is Flemish work of the late 17th or early 18th century. Beyond the Corridor is the former Chapel Balcony, with a small collection of English furniture. Here also hangs *(facing page, left)* Sir Joshua Reynolds' portrait of *Lady Caroline Price*, a fine example of his late work, painted in 1787. Lady Caroline was a daughter to the Earl of Tyrconnel and married to Sir Uvedale Price, the well-known amateur landscape-gardener, of Foxley, Herefordshire. Outstanding among the furniture is the Adam style cabinet *(facing page, right);* probably designed by one of Adam's numerous followers, it is of inlaid mahogany, with marquetry doors veneered in various woods—16 different varieties are used in this remarkable piece. The upper portion is fitted with pigeon-holes and small drawers, and a draw-out writing slide is fitted with inkwells and pen trays; *c.* 1768–1770 (Balcony). Also on the Balcony is the wine-cooler *(illustrated left, below)* made (probably by William France) to a design by Robert Adam for the dining room at Kenwood, Middlesex, the house he reconstructed and enlarged for Lord Mansfield, 1767–8. Descending the stairs and turning left across the Marble Hall, the visitor will find more English furniture on the Lower Corridor; here *(this page, above)* is the important triple-backed settee in the style of Chippendale, 1755–1760 in date; the seat is worked in petit-point with an outer margin in gros-point. It formerly belonged to a suite which has now been dispersed. Opposite the settee stands the inlaid mahogany bureau in the form of a globe; though not unique this style is very rare, and was also used for work-tables; it is English, *c.* 1812. Also on the Lower Corridor is the large collection of French Limoges enamels, mainly of 16th and 17th century date. These are painted on specially prepared sheets of thin copper, not the more familiar cloisonné. Depicting both religious and classical subjects, like the bronzes, an outstanding example of the former is the late 15th century plaque of *The Betrayal;* of the latter the 16th century plaque of *Aeneas fleeing from the Burning Troy*, from a series illustrating The Aeneid. One of the most important *(facing page, below right)* is the dish *The Judgement of Paris;* nearly 20″ in length, this magnificent dish is painted in grisaille, following a print by Marcantonio Raimondi after a painting by Raphael; the enamel was executed by Pierre Reymond, one of the better-known enamellers at Limoges, *c.* 1560, and bears his initials in the foreground. The even larger dish, *Allegory of the Old and New Testament*, with its confusing scene in continuous movement around a central boss, is also signed by Pierre Reymond. In coloured enamels are the four plaques from a set illustrating the months of the year. Right on the Lower Corridor is a part set of Indian chessmen in enamelled

gold; also cabinets of 16th century Turkish pottery, and late medieval and Renaissance wood-carvings. Particularly fine is the large triptych with *The Conversion of St. Hubert*, richly carved in boxwood (German, 16th century).

Right of the Lower Corridor is the room devoted to Brown Jack and other horses. Sir Harold Wernher's Brown Jack was one of the finest ever race-horses; foaled in 1924 by Jackdaw out of Querquidella, he won 25 races, including the Alexandra Stakes for six successive years, the Ascot Stakes, Goodwood Cup, Doncaster Cup, Ebor Handicap, Chester Cup, Hwfa Williams Memorial Stakes, Rosebery Memorial Plate, Prince Edward Handicap Plate, and the Salisbury Cup. His portrait by Sir Alfred Munnings *(above)*, and Lionel Edwards' drawings for the book are all here displayed. *Below* is the portrait *Charlottown* (by R. Stone Reeves), winner of the 1966 Derby and the Coronation Stakes (Epsom) 1967. There is also a portrait, by Raoul Millais, of Lady Zia Wernher's filly Meld, who in 1955 made racing history by winning the Thousand Guineas, the Oaks, the Coronation Stakes (Ascot), and the St. Leger. Meld was the great-grand-daughter of Double Life, the foundation mare of Lady Zia's stud, and has the further distinction to be the dam of Charlottown.

RIGHT: *The Emperor's Plate; this racing trophy, presented by Nicholas I of Russia between 1845 and 1853 in place of the Ascot Gold Cup, was won by Lord Albemarle's "Emperor" in 1845. In English silver, it represents Falconet's statue of Peter the Great overlooking the River Neva in St. Petersburg, mounted on a triangular base. (Russian Room)*

ABOVE: *Altdorfer's masterpiece*, Christ taking Leave of His Mother before the Passion, *one of Luton Hoo's finest pictures, shows the artist at the summit of his powers, and for long hung in a church in his native Ratisbon. The figures, although anatomically impossible, display an impressive grandeur with Christ standing majestically in their midst. The drama is heightened by the expansive mountain landscape and the stormy sky glimpsed through the ruined archway. At so late a date (c. 1522) the miniature group of the donor and his family appears an anachronism.*

NEC SPE
NEC METV
XXVII

The Main Gallery

The Main Gallery was formerly the private chapel at Luton Hoo, and was regularly used as such until 1940. The decorations here owe nothing to Sir Julius Wernher, as the chapel was designed by Street for the previous owner, John Gerard Leigh, during the 1870s. A great transformation has been effected to suit its present function, including the blocking of the stained glass windows and the covering of the tiled floor.

Here are displayed many of the finest things in the Collection—the Spanish, Italian and Flemish pictures, the Flemish tapestries, the Renaissance jewellery, and the Italian maiolica—all, with few exceptions, dating from the 15th to the 17th centuries.

There is no comparable private collection of Renaissance jewels in Britain. With few exceptions they date from the 16th and 17th centuries and are chiefly of Italian, Spanish and German origin. Jewels, the most personal works of art, unfortunately lose some of their interest when divorced from the costumes for which they were intended, or on which they appear as a feature of the design. That they were differently and more profusely worn by the rich in this period is evident from contemporary portraits. The jewels themselves evince that the emphasis was on colour, effected largely by enamelling the gold work, rather than sparkle—necessarily so, as the rose cutting of the diamond was not discovered until the end of the 17th century, and cabochon and table-cut stones will shine but hardly sparkle; they were often backed by coloured foil to enhance their brightness. For this purpose the diamond was less valued than coloured stones—rubies, emeralds and semi-precious stones of similar colour being especially favoured, with pearl-drops suspended from many jewels. The "baroque" pearl, not the polished pearl of modern times, was mostly used, and it has been suggested that the example forming the mermaid's body in the early 17th century German pendant is the finest although not the largest known.

The paintings offer a complete contrast. Compare Bermejo's *St. Michael* (*following page*) with Memlinc's small *Virgin and Child* (*facing page, top left*). Memlinc, Bermejo's Flemish contemporary, worked at Bruges between 1465 and 1494 and was scarcely influenced by the Renaissance. This small devotional panel, of moving simplicity, depicts the Mother concerned only with the Child, completely unaware of the onlooker. Like many of the ivories, it would have been an aid to the meditations of the medieval churchman and a small altarpiece.

The Italian picture (*facing page, below left*), *A Rest on the Flight into Egypt*, by Filippino Lippi (?1457–1504), is a charming example, where the youthful Mother gives cherries to the Child, while St. Joseph waters the ass in the background. The blue of the Virgin's robe is obtained from lapis-lazuli, a costly pigment signifying a commission from a rich patron.

St. Sebastian (*facing page, top right*); silver, parcel-gilt, 20″ high, this devotional piece was probably made at Augsburg to the design of Hans Holbein the Elder, and is related to a drawing from the artist's studio, now in the British Museum. The saint stands upon a reliquary depicting Our Lady of Pity, and a Latin inscription states that it was acquired by the Abbey of Kaisheim (Swabia) in 1497 by the Abbot Georg Kastner.

Facing page, below right is one of a pair of Italian maiolica dishes, from a service made at Castel Durante about 1519 for Isabella d'Este, Marchioness of Mantua. Encircling her arms are scenes from Ovid's *Metamorphoses*, in this instance the story of Apollo and Marsyas. This famous service is now dispersed among various collections.

This page, above, shows a Flemish tapestry of the early 16th century, depicting the Virgin and Child with Ss. Michael, John the Baptist, Jerome, and Francis of Assisi.

LEFT: *Illustrated here is one of the most important treasures, not only in the Main Gallery, but in Luton Hoo itself. This is the large and famous altarpiece of* St. Michael *by Bartolomé Bermejo, whose works are rarely seen outside his native Spain. It was painted* c. *1470-1471 under the influence of the Renaissance, as the altarpiece of the parish church of Tous (dedicated to St. Michael) near Valencia, where it remained until after 1864. It was subsequently purchased in Berlin by Sir Julius Wernher, and is probably the finest example of Spanish painting of that period in Britain. The saint, in golden armour and crimson-lined brocaded cope, all jewel-encrusted, stands, a glorious figure, on the monstrous dragon. The kneeling figure to the left is the unknown donor of the picture to its former home; his sombre robe and sallow face appear to enhance still further the splendour of the saint.*

ABOVE: *One of the splendid jewels in the collection is the dragon pendant. It is late 16th century Spanish work, the gold enamelled green and red for the creature's scales, and the head, body, and cartouches set with cabochon emeralds backed by green foil. In Spain such jewels were sometime presented to Christian shrines as votive offerings, but the history of this example is unknown.*

*

BACK COVER: *This aerial view, taken from the south, shows the house set in the park laid out in the 1760s and 1770s by "Capability" Brown, the famous landscape gardener of that period.*

SBN 85372 242 0